ISIS

Borgo Press Books Edited & Translated by FRANK J. MORLOCK

Alcestis: A Play in Five Acts, by Philippe Quinault * *Anna Karenina: A Play in Five Acts*, by Edmond Guiraud, from Leo Tolstoy * *Anthony: A Play in Five Acts*, by Alexandre Dumas, Père * *Atys: A Play in Five Acts*, by Philippe Quinault * *The Boss Lady: A Play in Five Acts*, by Paul Féval, Père * *The Children of Captain Grant: A Play in Five Acts*, by Jules Verne & Adolphe d'Ennery * *Cleopatra: A Play in Five Acts*, by Victorien Sardou * *Crime and Punishment: A Play in Three Acts*, by Frank J. Morlock, from Fyodor Dostoyevsky * *Don Quixote: A Play in Three Acts*, by Victorien Sardou, from Miguel de Cervantes * *The Dream of a Summer Night: A Fantasy Play in Three Acts*, by Paul Meurice * *Falstaff: A Play in Four Acts*, by William Shakespeare, John Dennis, William Kendrick, & Frank J. Morlock * *The Idiot: A Play in Three Acts*, by Frank J. Morlock, from Fyodor Dostoyevsky * *Isis: A Play in Five Acts*, by Philippe Quinault * *Jesus of Nazareth: A Play in Three Acts*, by Paul Demasy * *The Jew of Venice: A Play in Five Acts*, by Ferdinand Dugué * *Joan of Arc: A Play in Five Acts*, by Charles Desnoyer * *The Lily of the Valley: A Play in Five Acts*, by Théodore Barrière & Arthur de Beauplan, from Honoré de Balzac * *Lord Byron in Venice: A Play in Three Acts*, by Jacques Ancelot * *Louis XIV and the Affair of the Poisons: A Play in Five Acts*, by Victorien Sardou * *The Man Who Saw the Devil: A Play in Two Acts*, by Gaston Leroux * *Mathias Sandorf: A Play in Three Acts*, by Jules Verne & William Busnach * *Michael Strogoff: A Play in Five Acts*, by Jules Verne & Adolphe d'Ennery * *Les Misérables: A Play in Two Acts*, by Victor Hugo, Paul Meurice, & Charles Victor Hugo * *Monte Cristo, Part One: A Play in Five Acts*, by Alexandre Dumas, Père * *Monte Cristo, Part Two: A Play in Five Acts*, by Alexandre Dumas, Père * *Monte Cristo, Part Three: A Play in Five Acts*, by Alexandre Dumas, Père * *Monte Cristo, Part Four: A Play in Five Acts*, by Alexandre Dumas, Père * *The Musketeers: A Play in Five Acts*, by Alexandre Dumas, Père * *The Mysteries of Paris: A Play in Five Acts*, by Eugène Sue & Prosper Dinaux * *Napoléon Bonaparte: A Play in Six Acts*, by Alexandre Dumas, Père * *Ninety-Three: A Play in Four Acts*, by Victor Hugo & Paul Meurice * *Notes from the Underground: A Play in Two Acts*, by Frank J. Morlock, from Fyodor Dostoyevsky * *Outrageous Women: Lady MacBeth and Other French Plays*, edited by Frank J. Morlock * *Peau de Chagrin: A Play in Five Acts*, by Louis Judicis, from Honoré de Balzac * *The Prisoner of the Bastille: A Play in Five Acts*, by Alexandre Dumas, Père * *A Raw Youth: A Play in Five Acts*, by Frank J. Morlock, from Fyodor Dostoyevsky * *Richard Darlington: A Play in Three Acts*, by Alexandre Dumas, Père * *The San Felice: A Play in Five Acts*, by Maurice Drack, from Alexander Dumas, Père * *Saul and David: A Play in Five Acts*, by Voltaire * *Shylock, the Merchant of Venice: A Play in Three Acts*, by Alfred de Vigny * *Socrates: A Play in Three Acts*, by Voltaire * *The Son of Porthos: A Play in Five Acts*, by Émile Blavet, from M. Paul Mahalin * *The Stendhal Hamlet Scenarios and Other Shakespearean Shorts from the French*, edited by Frank J. Morlock * *A Summer Night's Dream: A Play in Three Acts*, by Joseph-Bernard Rosier & Adolphe de Leuwen * *Urbain Grandier and the Devils of Loudon: A Play in Four Acts*, by Alexandre Dumas, Père * *The Voyage Through the Impossible: A Play in Three Acts*, by Jules Verne & Adolphe d'Ennery * *The Whites and the Blues: A Play in Five Acts*, by Alexandre Dumas, Père * *William Shakespeare: A Play in Six Acts*, by Ferdinand Dugué * *The Youth of the Musketeers: A Play in Five Acts*, by Alexandre Dumas, Père

ISIS

A Play in Five Acts

by

Philippe Quinault

Translated and Adapted by Frank J. Morlock

THE BORGO PRESS

An Imprint of Wildside Press LLC

MMX

CONTENTS

DEDICATION

To

SUPAMAS SUKSAMRAN

CAST OF CHARACTERS

RENOWN

CHORUS OF FOLLOWERS OF RENOWN

RUMORS, UPROARS AND FIVE TRUMPETS, TWENTY-SIX FOLLOWERS OF RENOWN

NEPTUNE

FOLLOWERS OF NEPTUNE, TRITONS AND OTHER SEA GODS

SIX FLUTE PLAYING TRITONS

TWO SINGING TRITONS

TEN DANCING SEA GODS

APOLLO

FOLLOWERS OF APOLLO, THE NINE

MUSES AND LIBERAL ARTS

FIVE SINGING MUSES

CLIO

CALLIOPE

MELPOMENE

THALIA

URANIA

FOUR MUSES WHO PLAY INSTRUMENTS

TWO FLUTES BELOW

ERATO

EUTERPE

TWO VIOLINS BELOW

TERPSICHORE

POLYHYMNIA

THE SEVEN LIBERAL ARTS

HIERAX, lover of the nymph Io, and brother of Argus

PIRANTE, friend of Hierax

IO, nymph, daughter of the river Inachus, loved by Jupiter, persecuted by Juno, and finally received into the ranks of Celestial Divinities as Isis

MYCENE, nymph, confidante of Io

MERCURY

CHORUS OF EARTHLY DIVINITIES AND ECHOES

TROUPE OF DIVINITIES OF THE EARTH, THE OCEANS, AND SUBTERRANEAN RICHES

JUPITER

IRIS, Confidante of Juno

HEBE, daughter of Juno, and goddess of youth

CHORUS AND TROUPES of GAMES AND PLEASURES IN THE FOLLOWERS OF HEBE

CHORUS AND TROUPE OF NYMPHS IN THE FOLLOWERS OF JUNO

ARGUS

NYMPH, representing Syrinx

CHORUS AND TROUPE OF NYMPHS, COMPANIONS OF SYRINX

A WOODLAND CREATURE REPRESENTING THE GOD PAN

CHORUS AND TROUPE OF SHEPHERDS FOLLOWING PAN

CHORUS OF TROUPE OF SATYRS IN PAN'S FOLLOWING

CHORUS OF WOODLAND CREATURES, FOLLOWERS OF PAN

ERRINYS, A FURY

CHORUS AND TROUPE OF PEOPLES FROM FROZEN LANDS

TWO CONDUCTORS OF CHALYBYS WORKING TO FORGE STEEL

CHORUS AND TROUPE OF CHALYBYS

FOLLOWERS of FURIES, WAR, THE FURORS OF WAR, FAMINE, VIOLENT ILLS AND LANGUISHING ILLS, FIRE AND FLOODS, ETC.

THE THREE FATES (PARCAE)

CHORUS OF CELESTIAL DIVINITIES

CHORUS AND TROUPE OF THE PEOPLES OF EGYPT

PROLOGUE

The stage represents the Palace of Renown. It's open on all sides to receive news of important things done on earth, and what occurs that's memorable on the sea and that is discovered through mining. The divinity who presides in this palace appears, accompanied by his customary following, Rumors and Uproars who each bear a trumpet in hand and come from diverse parts of the world.

RENOWN AND THE CHORUS OF RENOWN, RUMORS, AND UPROARS:

Let's publish in all places
The triumphant valor of the greatest of heroes.
Let the earth and the heavens
Resound with the uproar of his dazzling glory.

RENOWN:

He's the one the gods have chosen
To complete the happiness of the French Empire;
Vainly, all unite, all conspire to trouble him.
It's in vain that *Envy* has leagued together so many kings.
Happy the Empire
Which follows his laws!

CHORUS: Happy the Empire
Which follows his laws!

RENOWN: All must necessarily admire him.
Let's speak of his virtues, let's tell of his exploits.
Hardly can all our voices
Suffice to do it.

RENOWN AND THE CHORUS:
Happy the Empire,
Which follows his laws.
It must be said,
Hundreds and hundreds of times,
Happy the Empire
Which follows his laws.

(Tritons and other Sea-gods accompany Neptune who emerges from the sea and enters the palace of Renown.)

TWO TRITONS: (singing)

It's the God of Waters who's going to appear.
Let's line up near our master.
Let's enchain the winds,
The most terrible of them.
Let the roar of the sea give way to our songs;
Reign, peaceful Zephyrs,
Bring back sweet Spring.
Flee far from here, cruel storms,
Nothing must trouble these shores.
Let's enchain the winds,
The most terrible of them, etc.

NEPTUNE: (speaking to Renown)

He's embellished my empire from the theatre to war;
Publish new exploits:
He's the same Conqueror, so famous on earth,
That triumphs again on the waves.

NEPTUNE:

Celebrate his great name on earth.

RENOWN:

Let's celebrate his great name on the ocean.

TOGETHER:

Let it not be bounded by the vastest seas.
Let it fly to the ends of the world.
Let it last as long as the universe.

CHORUS: (repeating the last five lines)

Let's celebrate his great name on earth.
Let's celebrate his great name on the ocean.
Let it not be bounded by the vastest seas.
Let it fly to the ends of the world.
Let it last as long as the universe.

CALLIOPE:

Cease, for a while, the terrible uproar of war
Which troubles the peace of a hundred diverse re-
gions.

CALLIOPE, CLIO, MELPOMENE, THALIA, AND URANIA:

Don't disturb the charms
Of our divine concerts.

(Erato, Euterpe, Terpsichore and Polyhymnia form
a concert of instruments.)

MELPOMENE:

Let's start our songs over,
Let's go make them heard
In an august court.

THALIA AND CALLIOPE:

Peace, sweet peace, doesn't dare to once again forbid
A celestial rest.

CALLIOPE, CLIO, MELPOMENE, THALIA AND URANIA:

Near the conqueror, let's go await
His very fortunate return.

(The Arts accompanying Apollo rejoice over the happiness this god is bringing them and making them anticipate.)

APOLLO: (speaking to Renown)

Don't always speak of cruel war.
Speak of pleasures and of games.
The Muses and The Arts are going to display their zeal,
I am going to favor their wishes.

We are preparing a new celebration
For the hero who calls them
To a happy asylum.
Don't always speak of cruel war.
Speak of pleasures and games.

RENOWN, NEPTUNE, APOLLO, THE MUSES AND THE CHORUS:

Let's not always speak of cruel war
Let's talk about pleasures and games.

RENOWN, NEPTUNE, APOLLO, THE MUSES, THE TRITONS, AND THE CHORUS OF RENOWN'S FOLLOWERS:

Hurry, pleasures, hurry.
Hurry to show your sweetest charms.

RENOWN:

It's still not time to believe
That these peaceful games won't be disturbed;
Nothing pleases the heroes who are assembled
more
Than to equal the exploits of eternal memory.
Enemies of peace: tremble.
You will soon see him race to Victory.
Your redoubled efforts
Will only serve to redouble his glory.

RENOWN, NEPTUNE, APOLLO, THE MUSES, THE TRITONS, AND THE CHORUS OF RENOWN'S FOLLOWERS:

Hurry, pleasures, hurry.
Hurry to show your sweetest charms.

While the Chorus sings and the instruments play, Neptune's followers dance with Apollo's followers and all these divinities go together to share the new celebration that the God of Parnassus has prepared with the Muses and The Arts.

CURTAIN

ACT I

The stage represents a pleasant prairie through which the river Inachus snakes.

HIERAX:

Let's stop loving an unfaithful woman.
Let's avoid the cruel shame
Of serving, of adoring one who no longer loves us.
Let's finish breaking the chains that she has broken.
Let's disengage ourselves, let's leave such a funereal empire.
Alas! Despite myself I am sighing.
Ah, my heart, what cowardice!
What charm remains in such a shameful martyrdom?
You aren't afraid of the fetters that cost us so

much,
Are you afraid of freedom?
Return, charming liberty,
You are only too diligent
If, in a heart, you make way for Love,
But how slow you are
When a just scorn urges your return.

PIRANTE: (entering)

It's too difficult to put up with your sad rumina-
tions.
Come, turn your steps toward these flowered
shores.
Look at these silver waves
That stray through these valleys
To make your enameled prairies shine.
Interrupt your sighs;
Everything ought to be calm here;
This beautiful abode is the asylum
Of repose and pleasure.

HIERAX:

Since an inconstant nymph
Has betrayed my love and failed in her word,
These parts, formerly so beautiful,
No longer have anything to enchant me.
The one I love has changed, and everything has

changed for me.

PIRANTE:

The daughter of Inachus loudly prefers you
To a thousand lovers jealous of your fate.
You have the support of her father,
The thousand cares of Argus, your brother,
Powerful Juno declares herself for you.

HIERAX:

If the ingrate still loved me, I would be her spouse.
This flighty nymph
Puts off from day to day
A marriage she once thought so sweet.
The inconstant no longer is hurried
By this burgeoning love which responded to mine.
Her change appears despite herself.
I know it only too well;
Her mouth sometimes says that she still loves me
But her heart, and her eyes no longer
Say anything to me about it.

PIRANTE:

Could she be dissimulating?
After so many oaths, you cannot suspect her?

HIERAX:

I no longer believe it very much, alas.
These oaths which were deceiving my tender and
credulous heart
Were made in these valleys, where through a thou-
sand detours
Inachus takes pleasure in prolonging his course.
It was on this charming shore
That his flighty daughter
Promised to love me forever.
The Zephyr was witness, Ocean was attentive
When the Nymph swore never to change.
But flighty Zephyr and fugitive Ocean
Ended by carrying away the oaths she made.
I see her, the infidel.

PIRANTE:

Clear things up with her.

(Io and Mycene enter.)

IO:

Do you love me? Can I flatter myself about it?

HIERAX:

Cruel one, how could you doubt it?

Vainly your inconstancy bursts out
Vainly it animates me to break all my fetters.
I still love you, ingrate:
More than you wish, and more than I wish.

IO:

I fear a funereal omen;
A devouring eagle just pounced before my eyes
On a bird that in this abode
Was entertaining me with a sweet warbling.
Put off our marriage, let's follow the advice of the
gods.

HIERAX:

Our marriage is displeasing only to your flighty
heart.
Answer me for yourself, I will answer to you for
the gods.
You once swore that this rebellious Ocean
Would make a new route to its source
Sooner than your heart would be seen to disengage.
Look at these waves spread through this vast plain,
It's the same inclination which always leads them.
Their course never changes, and you have changed.

IO:

Let me return to my secret terrors;

I expect this generous effort from your love.

HIERAX:

I want whatever pleases you, cruel though you are.
You are only abusing too much an unhappy heart.

IO:

No, I still love you.

HIERAX:

What extreme coldness!
Is this the way one ought to say one loves, inconstant one?

IO:

It's wrong for you to accuse me.
You've always seen your rivals scorned.

HIERAX:

The ill of my rivals doesn't equal my pain.
The sweet illusion of a vain hope
Doesn't make them fall from the reality of happiness.
None of them, like me, has lost your heart.
Like them, to your severe mood,
I am not accustomed.
What a torture to cease to please

When one has had the pleasure of being loved.
I sense only too well, that your heart is detaching
itself
And I don't know who's snatching it from me.
I search vainly for the happy lover
Who's robbing me of a charming blessing
Which I thought I alone pretended to.
I would feel my torture less
If I could find the one who is taking it from me.
You flee my looks, you tell me nothing.
I must free you of an annoying discussion.
My presence wounds you, and it too much con-
strains you.

IO:

Jealous, somber, and angry wherever I see you.
You never cease to complain.
I would like to love you as much as I ought
And you are forcing me to be afraid of you.

IO AND HIERAX:

No, it's only up to you
To render our fate sweeter.

IO:

No, it's only up to you
To render

My heart more tender.

HIERAX:

No, it's only up to you
To render my heart less jealous.

IO AND HIERAX:

No, it's only up to you
To render our fate sweeter.

(Hierax and Pirante leave.)

MYCENE:

This prince persists too long in his pain.
One can forgive the first distraction
Of a love which complains of being wronged
And which, mutinies unreasonably.
But in the end,
You torment yourself
Against a tormenting love.

IO:

I really want to speak to you at last without artifice.
This unfortunate Prince is alarming himself justi-
fiably.
The sovereign master of the earth and the heavens
Undertakes to please my eyes.

Love is offering me the empire of the heart of Jupiter.
Mercury came to tell me about it.
I see him descend from the clouds every day.
My heart resisted as much as it could
And to attack my constancy,
At least it took the greatest of the gods.

MYCENE:

One hears Jupiter sighing at one's ease.
He's a lover one dare not scorn,
And what's more, for great hearts glorious empire
Is difficult to refuse.

IO:

Then what urges me to surrender myself
To the attractions of a new love?
The more powerful the charm is, the more it would be in vain
To try to forbid it to me.
What, you want to leave me?
From where does this urgent care proceed?

MYCENE:

It's for you alone that Mercury is descending here.

(Exit Mycene.)

MERCURY: (from a cloud)

The powerful god who hurls thunder
And who holds the scepter of heaven in his hands
Has decided to come to earth
To drive away the evils that trouble humans.
Let the earth reply with care to this honor.
Echoes, resound in these attractive abodes;
Announce that today, for the happiness of the
world,
Jupiter is descending down here.

(The Chorus of Divinities of the Earth and the Chorus of Echoes repeat the last four verses as Mercury descends to the earth.)

MERCURY: (speaking to Io)

It's thus that Mercury,
To abuse some jealous gods,
Must speak loudly to all nature,
But he must explain himself otherwise to you.
It's for you, it's to please you
That Jupiter is descending from his celestial abode
And the blessings that his presence here is going to
bestow
Are only due to his love for you.

IO:

Why does this god want to descend from the high
heavens?
My vows are plighted, my heart has made a choice.
Love sooner or later can pretend
That all hearts are drawn up in formation under its
rule.
It's a homage that must be rendered,
But it's enough to render it once.

MERCURY:

It would be a strange constraint on loving
If a heart couldn't free itself for a better choice.
When it's for Jupiter the change is made,
It's not shameful to change.
Let the whole universe adorn itself
With the rarest things it has.
Let everything shine hereabouts
So that earth will share
The dazzle and glory of heavens.
Let all render homage
To the greatest of gods.

(The divinities of earth, waters and subterranean
riches come, magnificently adorned, to receive
Jupiter and to pay him homage.)

CHORUS OF DIVINITIES:

Let the earth share
The dazzle and glory of the heavens.
Let all render homage
To the greatest of gods.

(Twenty-four Singing Divinities. Eight Divinities
of the Earth. Eight Divinities of the Waters. Eight
Divinities of Subterranean Riches. A Dozen Dancing divinities. Four Divinities of the Earth, Four
Divinities of the waters. Four Divinities of Subterranean Riches.)

JUPITER: (descending from heaven)

The weapons that I hold protect innocence.
My power is fatal even to the pride of the titans.
You, who follow my laws, live under my power,
Always are happy, always satisfied.
Jupiter is coming to earth
To fulfill these blessings.
He's armed with thunder,
But that's to bring peace.

(The Chorus of divinities repeats these four verses
as Jupiter descends.)

CURTAIN

ACT II

Scene 1

The stage darkens with heavy clouds which sur-round it on all sides.

IO:

Where am I, where'd this cloud come from!
The waves of my father and his charming shore
Have suddenly vanished before my eyes!
Where can I find a passage?
The jealous Queen of Heaven,
Is she so soon making me pay the price
For pleasing the most powerful of Gods?
What do I see? What dazzle spreads through these
parts?

(Jupiter appears and the clouds which darkened the
stage are illuminated and painted with the most

brilliant and agreeable colors.)

JUPITER:

Let nothing astonish you, you are seeing Jupiter.
It's to deceive Juno and her jealous glances
That a cloud surrounds us.
Beautiful nymph, relax.
I love you and to tell you so
I am leaving my supreme empire with pleasure.
Lightning's in my hands, the gods pay me court,
I hold the whole universe obedient to me.
But if today I pretend
To engage your heart to love me in its turn,
I build my hopes less
On the grandeur of my power
Than on the excess of my love.

IO:

What's the use of your love choosing me here?
The honor comes to me too late; I've formed other
bonds.
I must fulfill my vows.
It wouldn't cost me any injustice
And wouldn't make for unhappiness.

JUPITER:

It's glory enough

For your first conqueror
To still be in your memory
And to struggle with me so long for your heart.

IO:

Glory must force my heart to defend itself.
If you are leaving heaven to seek the comforts
Of a tender love,
You could easily attack other hearts
Who would glory in surrendering.

JUPITER:

There's nothing in the heavens, there's nothing
here below,
With as much charm as your attractions;
Nothing can make me experience such a strong
passion.
Beautiful nymph, you carry it off
Over other beauties,
As much as Jupiter
Carries it off over other divinities.
Will you look on so much love with indifference?
What worry seizes you? Where are you turning
your steps?

IO:

In your presence

My heart offers too little resistance.
Alas, be content
With shocking my fidelity
And do not triumph over it.

JUPITER:

And why do you fear Jupiter who loves you?

IO:

I fear everything; I even fear myself.

JUPITER:

What, you want to flee me?

IO:

That's my last hope.

JUPITER:

Hear my love.

IO:

Hear my duty.

JUPITER:

You have a free heart and it can defend itself.

IO:

No, you won't leave my heart in your power.

JUPITER:

What, you won't listen to me?

IO:

It pains me so much not to want to.
Leave me alone.

JUPITER:

What, so soon?

IO:

I must at least wait.
Why didn't I flee before seeing you! Alas!

JUPITER:

Love solicits you for me.
And I see that you are leaving me.

IO:

Duty intends that I leave you
And I feel that you are stopping me.

MERCURY: (entering)

Iris is here below and Juno herself
Could be tracking you in these regions.

JUPITER:

For the nymph I love
I fear her furious distractions.

MERCURY:

If your love is surprised
Her vengeance will be funereal.

JUPITER:

Go, take care to stop Iris
My love will take care of the rest.

(Io tries to flee Jupiter who follows her off.)

MERCURY: (to Iris who entered)

Stop, beautiful Iris, delay for a moment,
Accomplishing Juno's wishes in these parts.

IRIS:

You can't have anything to say to me
And you are vainly stopping me.

MERCURY:

Why, if I told you that I intend to choose you
To attach my heart to an eternal chain?

IRIS:

Possibly I'd enjoy listening to you
But I'd have trouble believing you.

MERCURY:

Are you refusing to join your heart to mine?

IRIS:

Jupiter and Juno keep us constantly busy,
Our cares are great enough without Love injuring
us.
The two of us don't have the leisure to love well.

MERCURY:

If I made it my main business
To see you and please you?

IRIS:

I will make it my first duty
To please you and to see you.

MERCURY:

A faithful heart
Has charming attraction for me.
You have a thousand allures and you're not just
beautiful,
But I fear that you don't have
A faithful heart.

IRIS:

Why fear so much
That my heart will release itself?
I allow you to be unfaithful
As soon as I fly off.

MERCURY AND IRIS:

Promise me constant love;
I promise to love you forever.

MERCURY:

Let the dissimulation between us cease.

IRIS:

Today let's speak without mystification.

MERCURY AND IRIS:

The least artifice

Is offensive to love.

IRIS:

What care urges Jupiter to come down here?

MERCURY:

Only the benefit of mortals
Causes him to leave the heavens.
But what new suspicions can have seized Juno?
Isn't she following Jupiter to these parts?

IRIS:

Juno's just appeared in the garden of Hebe.

(Juno arrives in the midst of a cloud that comes forward.)

MERCURY:

A cloud opens to reveal her to my eyes.
Is this the way Iris speaks without mystification?
Is this the way I can be proud of her word?

IRIS:

Don't reproach me for not being sincere,
You aren't any more than I am.

MERCURY AND IRIS:

Keep for someone else
Your deceitful love.
I'm taking my heart back,
Take yours.

(The cloud nears the earth and Juno emerges.)

IRIS:

I've searched vainly for the daughter of Inachus.

JUNO:

Ah, I don't need to know any more.
No, Iris, let's not look for her any more.
Jupiter, in these parts, has given me offense.
I've traversed the air, I've pierced the cloud
That he positioned against my glance.
But vainly have I turned my eyes everywhere.
This god, with his supreme power,
Has hidden the nymph he loves from me,
And doesn't let me see anything but these strag-
gling troupes.
No, no, I am not a credulous spouse
That he can deceive so easily.
We shall see who dissembles better: Jupiter the
lover
Or jealous Juno.

He is master of the heavens, the earth is under his sway,
To his power all must bow,
But because he pretends only to arm himself with artifices,
Jupiter though he is, he's less strong than I.
In these isolated regions, see how beautiful the earth is.

IRIS:

It honors your master and shines beneath his feet.

JUNO:

Love, this unfaithful love,
That calls him from the heights of heaven
Makes everybody laugh at him down here.
With a new mistress
He finds attractions in the depths of deserts.
And heaven itself doesn't please him,
Or an immortal spouse.

JUPITER: (entering)

Today, in the gardens of Hebe, you must
Add a new nymph to your court;
What plan is so urgent that brings you to these parts?

JUNO:

I won't follow you any more
I am coming from your love to await a new care.
Don't be surprised that I leave you with pain,
And that I always have need of Jupiter.
You love me, I am certain of it.

JUPITER:

Just wish, I promise
That your wishes will be satisfied.

JUNO:

I've chosen a nymph and already the goddess
Of pleasant youth
Is preparing to receive her.
But without you, I don't dare to dispose of any-
body.
If I have some power
I don't pretend to more
Than your love gives me.
This gift from your hand will be precious to me.

JUPITER:

I approve of your wishes; let nothing thwart them.
Mercury, take care to please her.
And at her pleasure bring my orders in all parts

That all submit to the laws of the Queen of heaven.

MERCURY AND IRIS:

That all submit to the laws of the Queen of heaven.

JUPITER:

Speak, so that your choice is loudly declared.

JUNO:

The nymph who pleases me won't displease you.
You won't see her down here any more.
Of the greatest merit, neither the rarest beauty
The honors that I am preparing for her
Are not too much for her;
In short, Juno has chosen the daughter of Inachus.

JUPITER:

The daughter of Inachus!

JUNO:

Declare yourself for her.
Can you see in my suite a beautiful nymph
More capable of decorating my court,
And of testifying to me the care of your love?
You promised her to me and I demand her.

JUPITER:

You won't know how to fulfill a glory grand
enough
For the nymph you have chosen.
Juno commands,
Go, Mercury, obey.

IRIS:

Juno commands,
Go, Mercury, obey.

CURTAIN

ACT II

Scene 2

The scene changes and represents the gardens of Hebe, Goddess of Youth.

Hebe has a troupe of Games and Pleasures; Juno a troupe of nymphs in her suite. Six nymphs follow Juno. Twenty-four singing Games and Pleasures. Nine dancing Games and Pleasures. The Games and Pleasures dance forward towards Hebe.

HEBE:

The sweetest pleasures
Are made for youth.
Come, charming Games, come all;
Be very careful to bring with you

Strict Wisdom.
The sweetest of pleasures
Are made for youth.
Flee, flee, somber sadness,
Dark shames, flee far from us,
You are destined to terrify the old.
The sweetest of pleasures
Are made for youth.

(The Chorus repeats these last two verses.)

(The Games, The Pleasures, and Juno's nymphs divert themselves with dancing and singing while waiting for the new nymph who's going to be chosen by Juno.)

TWO NYMPHS: (singing together)

Love, profit in time;
Charming youth,
Satisfy your desires.
All laugh, all enchants,
In the most beautiful years.
Love brightens you,
March on her heels.
Seek to make for yourself
Fetters full of attractions.
What can please you
If you do not love?

Why do you fear to love
Inhuman beauties?
Stop worrying,
Love has its pains
Which must charm
The god that brightens you.
March on her heels,
Seek to make for yourself
Fetters full of attractions.
What can please you
If you don't love?

CHORUS:

How attractive these regions are.
Let's taste a bit of their charms;
Love never
Shed sad tears around here.
Cares and worries
Don't trouble its peace.
Let's rejoice in these retreats
With the most perfect of delights,
Follow us, charming pleasures
Fulfill all our wishes.
Let's observe these streams
In these laughing groves;
Sing little birds,
Sing about this foliage,

Join your soft warbling
To our new concerts.
Let's rejoice in these retreats
With the most charming of delights,
Follow us, charming pleasures
Fulfill all our wishes.

MERCURY AND IO: (enter escorting Io)

Serve, nymph, serve, with a faithful care
The powerful Queen of the Heavens.
Follow in these pleasant abodes,
Immortal youth
Please all, and all will laugh with her.

(Hebe and the nymphs receive Io.)

HEBE AND THE CHORUS OF NYMPHS:

What a charming pleasure it is
To be young and beautiful.
Let's triumph every moment
With a new conquest.
What a charming pleasure it is
To be young and beautiful.

CURTAIN

ACT III

The stage represents the isolated place where Argus lives, near a lake in the midst of a forest.

ARGUS:

In this solitary abode
You are under my guard, and Juno is leaving you here.
My eyes are watching one after the other
And observe you ceaselessly.

IO:

Is this the blessing Juno promised me?
Argus, tell me what crime I've committed.

ARGUS:

You are lovable,

Your eyes must charm less.
You are guilty of causing too much love.

IO:

Don't hide anything from me; of what does she accuse me?
What offense has made me so criminal in her eyes?
Am I incapable of appeasing her funereal wrath?

ARGUS:

It's a cruel offense
To appear beautiful
To the eyes of jealousy.
Jupiter's love for you showed itself too much.

IO:

O heaven! I am ruined if Juno is jealous.

ARGUS:

You don't please one spouse
If you are too pleasing to the other spouse.
You won't be able to do better
Than to be an ingrate and fly off.
You are leaving a faithful lover
To receive a more brilliant homage,
But this is an advantage
For which you'll pay dearly.

You won't be able to do better
Than to be an ingrate and steal off.
I am ordered to lock up your dangerous attractions.
The goddess forbids you to see anyone.

IO:

Jupiter is abandoning me to Juno's harshness.
No, Jupiter doesn't love me.

(Argus locks her in. Hierax enters and sees Io entering Argus's dwelling.)

HIERAX:

The perfidious one fears my presence,
She flees me in vain, I will go find her.

ARGUS: (stopping Hierax)

No.

HIERAX:

Let me reproach her
For her cruel inconstancy.

ARGUS:

No, you mustn't see her.

HIERAX:

What, Juno must thwart me?

ARGUS:

The order is precisely for everyone; give up a vain hope.

HIERAX:

Fraternal friendship has such little power?

ARGUS:

No, I know neither friend nor brother
I only know my duty.
Leave the nymph in peace here, she no longer loves you.

HIERAX:

Who is the happy lover that has made himself loved?
Name him to me.

ARGUS:

Tremble to hear him named.
It's an all powerful god, it's Jupiter himself.

HIERAX:

O Gods!

ARGUS:

Disentangle yourself from such a fatal love.
Without hesitation, you must resolve to do it,
It's a formidable rival,
A lover who hurls thunderbolts.

HIERAX:

All powerful gods! Ah, you were jealous
Of the happiness you ravished from me.
All powerful gods, you were jealous
Of seeing me happier than you.
You weren't able to endure the happiness of my life,
And I was observing your grandeurs without envy.
Loving her, I was loved, my fate was too sweet.
All powerful gods! Ah, you were jealous
Of the happiness you ravished from me.
All powerful gods! Ah, you were jealous
Of seeing me happier than you.

ARGUS:

Happy is he who can break his fetters!
Be done with a vain complaint.

Scorn infidelity.
Is an ungrateful heart worth the trouble
Of being so much regretted?
Happy is he who can break his fetters.

HIERAX AND ARGUS:

Happy is he who can break his fetters.

ARGUS:

Liberty, liberty.

(The Nymph Syrinx enters with a troupe of nymphs in hunting dress. Eight singing nymphs, companions of Syrinx. Four other singing nymphs. Six dancing nymphs, companions of Syrinx.)

SYRINX, CHORUS OF NYMPHS:

Liberty, liberty.

(One groups of nymphs dances while the others sing.)

ARGUS AND HIERAX:

What dances, what songs, and what novelty.

SYRINX AND THE NYMPHS:

If there's some good in the world
It's liberty.

ARGUS AND HIERAX:

What do you want?

CHORUS OF NYMPHS:

Liberty, liberty.

ARGUS AND HIERAX:

What do you want? You must answer us.

SYRINX AND THE NYMPHS:

If there's some treasure in the world
It's liberty.

(Enter troupes of Shepherds, Shepherdesses, Satyrs, and Woodland Creatures. Mercury enters.)

MERCURY, CHORUS OF NYMPHS, SHEPHERDS AND WOODLAND CREATURES):

Liberty, liberty.

MERCURY: (disguised as a shepherd, to Argus)

Pan cherishes the memory of the nymph, Syrinx.
Each day he still regrets her loss.
To celebrate a fest to her glory
This god himself, here assembles his court.
He intends there to be a touching spectacle
Representing the history of his love.

ARGUS:

That's a pleasure for us; go ahead, I consent to it.
I'm not opposed to innocent sports.

(Argus goes to sit on a chair on the lawn near the place where Io is shut up, and makes Hierax sit on the other side.)

MERCURY: (speaking aside to the troupe he's leading)

He's in the trap, finish up without stopping.
Complete the surprise of Argus and all his eyes.
If you attempt a great enterprise
Mercury will lead you, Love will favor you
And you will serve the most powerful gods.

(Mercury, and the Shepherds, Satyrs and Woodland creatures withdraw towards the back of the stage.)

SYRINX AND THE CHORUS OF NYMPHS:

Liberty, liberty
If there's some treasure in the world,
It's liberty, liberty.

SYRINX:

The empire of Love is no less agitated

Than the empire of the Ocean.
Don't seek any other happiness
Than sweet leisure in profound peace.

SYRINX AND THE CHORUS:

If there's some treasure in the world
It's liberty.
Liberty, liberty.

(As one group of nymphs sings, the rest dance.)

(Shepherds and Sylvan creatures come to offer presents of fruits and flowers to the nymph Syrinx and try to persuade her not to go on the hunt and to stay under the rule of Love.)

TWO SHEPHERDS:

What blessing must you be expecting,
Beauties who hunt in these parts?
What can you take,
What is a tender heart worth
That submits to your laws?
It's only in loving
That one finds a strong charm.
Love, in the end, in your turn.
All must give in to Love.
Love knows how to strike a sure blow to
The flighty stag who flees in vain.

Even in the secret caverns,
In the depths of the forest,
All must feel Love's darts.
When love calls you,
Why do you flee his pleasures?
The newborn Rose
Is no less beautiful
For loving Zephyrs.
It's only in loving
That one finds a strong charm.
Even in the secret caverns,
In the depths of the forests,
All must feel Love's darts.

PAN:

I love you, charming nymph;
An immortal lover seeks to be pleasing to your
eyes.

SYRINX:

Pan is a powerful god; I revere the gods
But the name of lover appalls me.

PAN:

To make you find the name of lover softer,
I will join the title spouse.
I won't have any bother

To entangle myself
In a lovable fetter.
I won't have any bother
To entangle myself
So as never to stray.
Love a god who adores you.
Let's join together in a charming bond.

SYRINX:

A spouse is even
More to be feared than a lover.

PAN:

Dissolve vain alarms,
Experience love and its charms,
Know its sweetest attractions.
No, it can't be possible,
That from want of knowing it,
It won't please you.

SYRINX:

The misfortunes of others render me wise.
Ah! What misfortune
To let your heart be attached?
Why must you spend the most beautiful time of
your life
In a mortal languor?

Ah! What misfortune!
Why not have the courage
To free yourself from the harshness
Of a funereal slavery?
Ah! What a misfortune
To let your heart be attached.

PAN:

Ah, what a shame
For you not to know love!
What's the use of having so many attractions for
your share,
If you neglect the greatest advantage?
What's the use of knowing every way to charm?
Ah! What a shame
For you not to know how to love!

**CHORUS OF WOODLAND CREATURES,
SATYRS AND SHEPHERDS**:

Love without stopping.

CHORUS OF NYMPHS:

We never love.

**CHORUS OF WOODLAND CREATURES,
SATYRS and SHEPHERDS**:

Let's give in to love which urges us

To live happily, love without stopping

CHORUS OF NYMPHS:

To live in peace,
Let's never love.

SYRINX:

Pain always follows hearts that Love wounds.

PAN:

Calm wisdom
Has only imperfect pleasures.

CHORUS OF WOODLAND CREATURES, SATYRS, AND SHEPHERDS:

Let's love without stopping.

CHORUS OF NYMPHS:

Let's never love.

SYRINX:

You can't love without weakness.

PAN:

How many attractions this weakness has!

CHORUS OF WOODLAND CREATURES, SATYRS AND SHEPHERDS:

Let's love without stopping.

CHORUS OF NYMPHS:

Let's never love.

CHORUS OF WOODLAND CREATURES, SATYRS, AND SHEPHERDS:

Let's give in to Love which urges us
To live happily, let's love without stopping.

CHORUS OF NYMPHS:

To live in peace,
Let's never love.

SYRINX:

Must such a fine day be spent in idle discourse?
My companions, let's run in the thickest part of the
forest.
See that before us it's showing the best of its features.
Let's run to the hunt.

CHORUS:

Let's run to the hunt.

SYRINX: (returning on stage after running out, followed by Pan)

Why are you following me so close?

PAN:

Why do you flee the one who loves you?

SYRINX:

A lover gets in my way.

SYRINX AND THE CHORUSES: (offstage)

Let's run to the hunt.

(Syrinx runs off again, followed by Pan. After a moment Pan reenters, still following Syrinx.)

PAN:

I can't leave you, my heart's bound to you
By the strongest and softest chains.

SYRINX:

My companions, come! It's in vain that I call.

PAN:

Listen, ingrate, listen.
A god, charmed by your beauties,

Who swears an eternal, faithful love—

SYRINX: (fleeing)

I declare immortal war on Love.

TROUPE OF SHEPHERDS: (stopping Syrinx)

Cruel one, stop.

TROUPE OF SATYRS AND WOODLAND CREATURES: (stopping Syrinx)

Stop, cruel one.

SYRINX:

You are retaining me at all cost.

CHORUS OF SATYRS, WOODLAND CREATURES AND SHEPHERDS:

Cruel one, stop.

SYRINX:

Gods, protectors of innocence,
Naiads, nymphs of these streams,
I implore your assistance here.

(Syrinx throws herself in the waters.)

PAN: (following Syrinx into the lake where she

has hurled herself)

To what are you exposing yourself? What new prodigies?
The nymph's been changed into roses?

(The wind rushes through the roses and makes them utter a plaintive sound)

Alas! What noise! What do I hear? Ah, what new voices!
The nymph is trying to express her regrets.
How sweet her murmur is! How attractive is her complaint.
Let's not cease complaining with her.
Let's reanimate the charming remains
Of a nymph who was so beautiful.
She's still responding to our laments.
Let's not cease complaining with her.

(Pan gives the roses to shepherds, to Satyrs, and to Woodland creatures who form a concert with flutes.)

PAN:

The eyes that charmed me will never see day any more.
Was it thus, cruel Love
That you must avenge yourself on a rebellious

beauty?
Wouldn't it have sufficed to render yourself con-
queror
And to see her insensitive heart in your fetters,
Burning with mine in an eternal passion?
Let all feel my torments.

PAN AND TWO SHEPHERDS: (accompanied
by a concert of flutes)

Let's revive the charming remains
Of a nymph who was so beautiful.
She's still responding to our laments.
Let's not stop from complaining with her.

(Argus begins to sigh, Mercury disguised as a
shepherd approaches him and ends by putting him
to sleep by touching him with his caduceus.)

PAN:

Let these plaintive roses be forever loved.

MERCURY:

It suffices, Argus is asleep, all his eyes are shut.
Let's go, let nothing delay us.
Let's free the nymph he's guarding.

(Mercury bringing Io out of Argus' dwelling which
he opens with a tap from his caduceus.)

MERCURY:

Recognize Mercury and flee with us.
Distance yourself from Argus before he awakes.

HIERAX: (stopping Io and speaking to Mercury)

Argus with his hundred eyes snoozes.
But do you think
To put a jealous lover to sleep?
Stay.

MERCURY:

Wretch, where'd you get this audacity from?

HIERAX:

I've lost everything;
I await death without fear.
A thunderbolt is a mercy
For an unfortunate like me.
Wake up, Argus, you are letting yourself be surprised.

ARGUS AND HIERAX:

Powerful queen of heaven,
Juno, come to our defense.

MERCURY: (striking Argus and Hierax with his caduceus)

Begin to feel the wrath of the gods.

(Argus falls dead and Hierax changes into a bird of prey and flies off.)

CHORUS OF WOODLAND CREATURES AND SHEPHERDS:

Let's get out of here!

IO:

If you leave me, what help can I expect?

CHORUS OF WOODLAND CREATURES, SATYRS AND SHEPHERDS:

Let's get out of here! Juno's coming to these parts.

(Juno enters in her chariot, followed by the Errinys and Furies.)

JUNO:

See the light of day again, Argus, let your appearance change.

(Argus is transformed into Paon and takes up a place before Juno's chariot.)

JUNO:

And you, nymph, learn how Juno avenges herself.
Emerge, barbarous Errinys, emerge from the
depths of Hell.
Come, take care to serve my fatal vengeance,
And to reveal its horror in a hundred different re-
gions.
Shock the whole universe
With the tortures of my rival.
Come punish her to my wrath's taste
Increase your infernal rage
And make it, if it's possible, equal to
The fury of my jealous heart.

(The Fury emerges from Hell, she pursues Io, she
carries her off and Juno returns to Heaven.

IO: (pursued by the fury)

O gods! To what have you reduced me?

CURTAIN

ACT IV

Scene 1

The scene represents the iciest region of Scythia.

People appear transfixed with cold.

CHORUS OF PEOPLE OF FROZEN RE-GIONS: (singing)

Winter that torments us
Is determined to freeze us.
We don't know how to speak
Except in a shivering voice.
Snow and icicles
Are giving us mortal shakes,
Frost spreads
Over our torpid bodies,
The cold chills our senses,

The hardest rocks are split.
Snow and icicles
Give us mortal shakes.

IO: (pursued by the Fury enters)

Leave me alone, cruel Fury.
Cruel one, let me breathe for a moment.
Ah, barbarian, the more I beg you,
The more you take pleasure in increasing my torture.

FURY:

Sigh, shiver, weep, scream, I am making a charming spectacle of your pain for myself.

IO:

Leave me alone, cruel Fury.
Cruel one, let me breathe for a moment.
What a horrible abode! What unbearable cold!
Your serpents animated by your implacable rage,
Aren't they cruel enough, executioner?
To punish a miserable heart,
Are you coming so far to find new tortures?

FURY:

Unfortunate inhabitants of a frightful residence,
Know Juno's funereal wrath

Through her harsh vengeance.
You are looking at an unfortunate
Who's suffering a hundred time more than you.

(Io and the Fury repeat the last two lines.)

CHORUS OF PEOPLE OF FROZEN RE-GIONS:

To tremble from torpor in the horror of frosts!

IO:

Ah, what pain
To endure so many wrongs without finding death!
Ah! What inhuman vengeance.

THE FURY:

Come, change tortures, move on to other regions.

(The Fury drags Io and carries her off.)

IO:

Ah, what pain!

CHORUS OF PEOPLE OF FROZEN RE-GIONS:

Ah, what pain!
To tremble with torpor in the horrors of frost!

ACT IV

Scene 2

The scene changes and represents on two sides the forges of Chalybys who work at forging steel; the Sea appears in the hollow. Eight dancing Chalybys, Two Conductors of singing Chalybys. Chorus of Chalybys. As several Chalybys work at the forges, others come and go hurriedly to bring steel from the mines and to remove what is necessary from work that is completed.)

THE TWO CONDUCTORS AND THE CHORUS OF CHALYBYS:

How the fire of the forges glows.
Let's work with renewed effort,
So as to make the anvil echo

Under heavy blows of hammers.

(Io appears amidst the fires which emerge from the forges.)

IO:

What deluge of fire is coming to spread over me?
O heaven!

(The Chalybys pass by Io with parts of swords and lances and hatchets half forged.)

THE FURY:

Heaven can't hear you.
You're not wailing loud enough.

THE TWO CONDUCTORS AND THE CHORUS OF CHALYBYS:

Let them prepare all that must be done.

IO:

Juno will be less inhumane;
You make me suffer too much;
You serve her hate too well.

THE FURY:

To the taste of her scornful jealousy
Your most cruel ills will still be too soft.

IO:

Alas! What extreme harshness.
It's in vain that Jupiter loved me.
Juno's hate rejoices in my torture.
How powerfully you hate,
Great gods, would that you love the same!

(The fires from the forges increase, and the Chalybys surround Io with pieces of steel and burnings.)

IO:

Can't I just cease to live?
Let's seek death in the waves.

FURY:

Everywhere, my rage must follow you.
Expect neither help not repose.

(Io flees and runs to the top of as rock, from which
she throws herself into the sea, the Fury throws
herself after the nymph.)

CURTAIN

ACT IV

Scene 3

The scene changes and represents the cavern of the Parcae. The followers of the Parcae. The Furors of War, Violent and Languishing Maladies, Famine, Fire, Flood, and Singers and Dancers.

CHORUS OF THE FOLLOWERS OF THE PARCAE:

Let's execute the decree of Fate,
Let's follow its cruelest laws.
Let's present without stopping
New victims to death.

WAR:

Let the sword—

FAMINE:

Let hunger—

FIRE:

Let flames—

FLOOD:

Let water—

ALL TOGETHER:

Let all serve to excavate thousands and thousands
of tombs.

THE VIOLENT ILLNESSES:

Let all rush to enter the somber kingdoms
By a thousand different paths.

THE LANGUISHING ILLNESSES:

Get it over with by expiring, unfortunate terminally
ill,
Seek a long rest in the dwelling of shades.

CHORUS:

Let's execute the decree of Fate.
Let's follow its cruelest laws.
Let's present without cease,

New victims to death.

WAR:

Let the sword—

FAMINE:

Let hunger—

FIRE:

Let fires—

FLOOD:

Let water—

ALL TOGETHER:

Let all serve to excavate thousands and thousands
of tombs.

(The followers of the Parcae exhibit pleasure when
she puts an end to the fate of humans.)

(Enter Io pursued by the Fury.)

IO: (speaking to the Followers of the Parcae)

It's against me that you must turn
Your most funereal rigor.
Tear me from the remainder of an odious life.

Hasten to end it.

CHORUS OF THE FOLLOWERS OF THE PARCAE:

That's up to the Parcae to order.

IO:

Favor my wishes, Sovereign goddesses,
Who rule by Destiny's immutable laws.
End my days and my sufferings.
Don't condemn me to die a thousand times.

(The depths of the cavern open and the Three Parcae emerge.)

THE THREE PARCAE:

The thread of life
Of all humans,
Following our wish,
Twists in our hands.

IO:

Cut my sad fate with a blow which will deliver me
From the tortures that Juno constrains me to suffer.
Each prays to you for life,
And I pray to you to die.

THE FURY:

Jupiter has submitted her to the sway of his spouse.
She made Juno jealous.
The love of a powerful god knew how to charm
her.
She's been too little punished as yet.

IO:

Is it such a great crime to love
The one all the universe adores?

THE PARCAE:

Nymph, appease Juno if you wish to see the end
Of your deplorable fate.
That's the decree of Destiny.
It is irrevocable.

IO:

Alas, how to bend an implacable hate?

**THE PARCAE, THE CHORUS OF THE FOL-
LOWERS OF THE PARCAE**:

That's the decree of Fate.
It is irrevocable.

CURTAIN

ACT V

The stage represents the shores of the Nile, and one of the mouths through which this river enters the sea. Io emerges from the sea, from which she is pulled by the Fury.

IO:

End my torments, powerful Master of the world,
Without you, without your love, alas!
I wouldn't be suffering,
Reduced to despair, dying, vagabond.
I've born my torture in a thousand frightful climes,
A horrible Fury attached to my heels
Has followed me across the vast breast of the
Ocean.
End my torments, powerful master of the world.
See with what misfortunes

Your spouse is punishing my unlucky attractions down here.
From pity, open the gates of death,
End my torments, powerful master of the world.
Without you, without your love, alas!
I wouldn't be suffering.
It's Jupiter who loved me! Hey, who could believe it?
I am no longer in his memory.
He doesn't hear my screams, he doesn't see my tears.
After having delivered me to the cruelest misfortunes,
He's calm in the summit of Glory.
He abandons me in the midst of sorrows.
In the end, I am succumbing, happy if I die.

(Io falls, overwhelmed with her torments, and Jupiter, touched with pity descends from heaven.)

JUPITER:

I'm not allowed to end your pain,
And my sovereign power
Must follow Destiny's irrevocable law.
All that I can do through extreme love
Is to leave heaven and my supreme glory,
To take part in the ills that you are suffering for

me.

IO:

Ah! My torture increases still.
All the fires of Hell are burning me and devouring me.
Will I die so many times without seeing my fate end?

JUPITER:

My tenderness for you makes Juno inflexible.
She sees my love, it seems too strong for her.
Her wrath increases and becomes invincible.

IO:

Never mind, always be sensitive in my favor.

JUPITER:

It's too much to expose you to her jealous distraction.
By loving you I excite her terrible vengeance.

IO:

Love me, if it is possible for you,
Enough to force her to give me death.

(Juno descends to earth.)

JUPITER:

Come, pitiless goddess,
Come, look, recognize
This dying nymph once too lovable.
It's enough to punish her, it's enough to avenge
yourself,
The dazzle of her beauty doesn't make her more
guilty;
Through the horror of the torture which over-
whelms her,
Her crime and her attractions are effaced together.
Without jealousy and without storms
See her eyes drowned in tears,
Let the shadow of death begin to cover her.

JUNO:

There are still too many charms
That know how to soften you up.

JUPITER:

Can a just pity aggravate you?
Your fatal wrath ought to die out.

JUNO:

Ah! You pity her too much, she isn't complaining.
No, she cannot suffer too much.

JUPITER:

I know that it is on you her fate depends.
It's only on your bounty that she must have recourse.
There's nothing from me you cannot expect,
If I can oblige your hate to give over.

IO:

Ah, let me die.

JUPITER:

Take care to help her.

JUNO:

You love her with a love too tender.
No, she cannot suffer too much.

JUPITER:

What, the heart of Juno, as great as it may be.
Doesn't know how to triumph over an unjust furor?

JUNO:

On earth and in heaven, Jupiter is the master.
And Jupiter is not the master of his heart?

JUPITER:

Well, it's necessary that I begin
To conquer myself today.

JUNO:

You will learn to conquer me in my turn.

JUPITER:

Abandon your vengeance.
I return my love to you.

JUNO:

I will abandon my vengeance.
Will you return to me your love?

JUPITER:

Black waves of Styx, it's by you I swear,
Horrible river, hearken to the oath I am taking.
If this nymph ever resumes all her allures,
If Juno stops all the torments she's enduring,
I swear that her eyes will trouble me no further.
Our hearts reunited in happy peace,
Black waves of Styx, it's by you I swear,
Horrible river, hearken to the oath I am taking.

JUNO:

Nymph, I intend to end your cruel suffering.
Let the Fury take with her back to Hell,
The trouble and horrors with which you feel your-
self seized.

(The Fury is thrust back into Hell and Io finds herself freed from her sufferings.)

JUNO:

After a strict torture,
Taste the perfect blessings that the gods have cho-
sen,
And, under the new name of Isis,
Rejoice in a happiness that will never end.

JUPITER AND JUNO:

Gods, receive Isis into the ranks of the immortals.
Nations neighboring the Nile, erect altars to her.

(The divinities of heaven descend to receive Isis,
the people of Egypt erect an altar to her and recognize her as the divinity who must protect them.
Four female Egyptian singers. The people of Egypt
as dancers. Four Egyptian dancing girls.)

CHORUS OF DIVINITIES:

Come, new divinity.

CHORUS OF THE PEOPLE OF EGYPT:

Isis, turn your eyes toward us,
Observe the passion of our zeal.

CHORUS OF DIVINITIES:

The Celestial Court is calling you.

CHORUS OF THE PEOPLE OF EGYPT:

All revere you in these parts.

(Jupiter and Juno take their place in the midst of the Divinities and make room for Isis.)

JUPITER AND JUNO:

Isis is immortal.
Isis is going to shine in the heavens.
Isis enjoys with the gods
An eternal glory.

(Jupiter, Juno and the divinities return to heaven and lead Isis, while the Chorus of Divinities and The People of Egypt repeat the last four verses.)

CURTAIN

ABOUT FRANK J. MORLOCK

FRANK J. MORLOCK has written and translated many plays since retiring from the legal profession in 1992. His translations have also appeared on Project Gutenberg, the Alexandre Dumas Père web page, Literature in the Age of Napoléon, Infinite Artistries.com, and Munsey's (formerly Black-mask). In 2006 he received an award from the North American Jules Verne Society for his translations of Verne's plays. He lives and works in México.

www.ingramcontent.com/pod-product-compliance
Lightning Source LLC
LaVergne TN
LVHW011214080426
835508LV00007B/786